JACKIE KAY

LIFE MASK

BLOODAXE BOOKS

Copyright © Jackie Kay 2005

ISBN: 1 85224 691 X

First published 2005 by
Bloodaxe Books Ltd,
Highgreen,
Tarset,
Northumberland NE48 1RP.

www.bloodaxebooks.com
For further information about Bloodaxe titles
please visit our website or write to
the above address for a catalogue.

Bloodaxe Books Ltd acknowledges
the financial assistance of
Arts Council England, North East.

Cover printing by J. Thomson Colour Printers Ltd, Glasgow.

Printed in Great Britain by
Bell & Bain Limited, Glasgow, Scotland.

£7.95

LIFE MASK

Jackie Kay was born and brought up in Scotland. Her first collection, *The Adoption Papers* (Bloodaxe Books, 1991), tells the story – her story – of a black girl's adoption by a white Scottish couple. It received a Scottish Arts Council Book Award, a Saltire First Book of the Year Award and a Forward Prize in 1992, and was also shortlisted for the *Mail on Sunday* / John Llewellyn Rhys Prize. She won a Somerset Maugham Award for her second collection, *Other Lovers* (Bloodaxe Books, 1993), and she has won the Signal Poetry Award twice – in 1993 and 1999 – for her books of poetry for children, *Two's Company* (Blackie, 1992) and *The Frog Who Dreamed She Was an Opera Singer* (Bloomsbury, 1998).

In 1998, Bloodaxe published her third collection, *Off Colour*, a Poetry Book Society Special Commendation, which was shortlisted for the T.S. Eliot Prize, as well as a selection of her work on *The Poetry Quartets: 1*, the first poetry cassette in the British Council/Bloodaxe Books series. Her first novel, *Trumpet* (Picador, 1998), won the Guardian Fiction Prize, a Scottish Arts Council Book Award and the Author's Club first novel award. In 2002 her first book of stories, *Why Don't You Stop Telling Stories*, appeared from Picador, and her first novel for children, *Straw Girl*, from Macmillan. Her latest collection of poems is *Life Mask* (Bloodaxe Books, 2005), a Poetry Book Society Recommendation.

She has written widely for stage and television, and lives in Manchester with her son.

She is a Fellow of the Royal Society of Literature and teaches Creative Writing at Newcastle University.

for my son Matthew, my rock,
with love

NOTE & ACKNOWLEDGEMENTS

Some of these poems have appeared in the *TLS*; others have been broadcast on BBC Radio 3 and 4. BBC Radio 4 commissioned 'Piano 4 P.M.' and 'Childhood, Still' for National Poetry Day. The Open University commissioned 'There's Trouble for Maw Broon'.

Having a bronze head of me made by the sculptor Michael Snowdon inspired the sequence of poems about the life mask. (My head is one of twelve herms in Edinburgh Business Park.) Michael talked to me about the whole process, which I found fascinating. I sat for him for twenty hours. Michael said things like 'clay has no personality' or 'clay is freedom' or 'plaster is unforgiving'. It sparked off a series of poems, which were then put to music by the Spontaniacs and performed at the Edinburgh Jazz Festival.

'Pencil, Knife' was inspired by the experience of being drawn by the Scottish artist, Joyce Cairns. 'Mirror, Mirror' and 'The Staging of My Body' were inspired by the work of Helen Chadwick and commissioned by the Barbican Arts Centre.

I would like to thank Linda Anderson and Anne Spencer for lending me their cottage in East Woodburn. Thank you also to Becky and Jeremy Hardy for lending me the manse house in Metton to write in. Thanks to the Scottish Arts Council, and the British Council of Nigeria.

Without friends, whaur would we be? My thanks to my very good friends: Amanda Dalton, Julia Darling, Maura Dooley, Nick Drake, Liz Lochhead and Ali Smith.

I am grateful to the Society of Authors for a Cholmondeley Award.

CONTENTS

Late Love

How they strut about, people in love,
how tall they grow, pleased with themselves,
their hair, glossy, their skin shining.
They don't remember who they have been.

How filmic they are just for this time.
How important they've become – secret, above
the order of things, the dreary mundane.
Every church bell ringing, a fresh sign.

How dull the lot that are not in love.
Their clothes shabby, their skin lustreless;
how clueless they are, hair a mess; how they trudge
up and down streets in the rain,

remembering one kiss in a dark alley,
a touch in a changing-room, if lucky, a lovely wait
for the phone to ring, maybe, baby.
The past with its rush of velvet, its secret hush

already miles away, dimming now, in the late day.

Glen Strathfarrar

I don't know if I can go with you to Glen Strathfarrar
Where time has stopped for over a hundred years
And the proud red deer looks down on our fears,

Where you loved me once and had me drink fresh stream water
From your delicate cupped hands, if I can bear
The stock-still beauty after all these years.

Skyscraper

Where there is love, love is never wasted.
Wasted love like wasted food feeds nobody.

It groans down a chute; lands in the gutter;
hear the last words of wasted love mutter.

Dar pump sweet kin heart ling,
a mush of sweet singing, baby, baby, baby.

In the dark, wasted love grows fungi,
in the peat dank, at the chute end.

The last munch, slobber, screech, scrunch.
The last whine, whinge, yobby gob shine.

But oh when love is not wasted, love deep-down
crawls towards the moors under a neep moon.

The Spare Room

When my lover found a brand-new lover,
on the longest day of the year by far,
she asked if I would move into the spare room.

That first night I was awake and then asleep,
and then awake, very hot and very cold;
I turned and tossed in the small white room.

Halfway through the night, still black outside,
the air held its chilly breath and I held my head,
wide, wide awake in the pale spare room.

After a long, long while daylight spilled.
I climbed out of the spare room bed.
I stood staring at the bed, at the dented pillows.

Last night I must have turned from her side to mine
from the blank wall to the blind window, spoon to moon,
as if two people had slept in the spare room bed.

There's Trouble for Maw Broon

It dawned on me, aw of a sudden
the sickening reason Paw wis changing.
I'd been the mug. I didnae want tae face
whit was staring me in the face.
It crept up on me bit by bit,
till wan sudden day I saw Paw wis fit.
He'd had his tash clipped neatly.
He'd toyed wey the thocht o' a toupe, he telt me.
Really! He bought a brand new bunnet.
I couldnie hack it, the way he wore it.
There wis ither clues as weel
noo I come tae play back the reel.
He stapped drinking spilt tea
frae his saucer; he didnae belch and say
Guid fir me! He didnae tut at the TV.
If he dribbled he wiped his chin.
If he coughed he covered his mooth.
He chucked oot his auld tackety boots.
He threw oot his pipe and his baccie.
He lost interest in fitba.
He started eating his veggies raw.
It wis mair than I coud staund.
I'd find masell at the sink wey shaking haunds.
He wisnae a skinflint anymair.
He spent a wee fortune on a pair
o good leather shoes, a mint on a new jaicket.
I couldnie take it. I couldnie fake it.
Then he fixed oor shoogly table.
That wis it! I'd had my fill.
I wis on tae him. Guilt! Pure and simple.
Wiring plugs. Cleaning oor auld quilt.
I wis able tae see it clear as day.
There wis a fierce jalous wind blowing that day.
Bitter and bleak and bad like my thoughts.
This wis final. This wis ma lot.
I wis dreary and dowdy and dull
Sic tae the back teeth wey masell
and Paw wis looking swell,
aw spruced up and smelling o' Old Spice.

I wis finally sure, knew in a trice.
I wisnae going round the bend
efter a', I wisnae oot o' my mind,
I wisnae telling mysell wee lies,
I wisnae suspicious and paranoid.
Paw wis late hame eight nichts in ten.
He wisnae wan o' they drinking men.
I couldnie run from the truth anymair.
I'd had it up tae here.
I ken the truth, it's the truth I ken
Paw's been hauving it aff in oor but n' ben
under oor wee frail tin roof
in oor special place when – s'truth
efter a' we've been through thegither
through rain and stormy weather,
oor sacred but n' ben
oot o' toon fir a lang weekend.
I could staund maist onything
but no the thought o' oor but n ben.
It's spoilt noo. Ruined. Dirty.
Paw's been underhaund. Shifty.
I canny go tae ma wee haven.
I'm mental. Raving.
When I think o' me and Paw Broon,
how we slept the nicht thegither like spoons,
and noo, the dirty swine!
That braw wee place wis mine, mine.

Spoons

We two sleeping like spoons,
under the bowl of moon,
gone soon, gone soon
quine and loon.

We two sleeping like spoons,
humming our silver tune
deep doon, deep doon
quine and loon.

Rusted, the sleeping spoons,
under the empty moon
scrap soon, scrap soon
quine and loon.

Mugs

The last bit of civilisation happened in the kitchen,
where, however much you were bitching at me or me you,
I still asked you if you wanted a cup of tea or coffee
and you, occasionally, not so often, asked me.

For some reason, perhaps living in England a long while,
it consoled me: at least we still boil the kettle
and shout 'your tea's ready!' At least we still – small mercy.
Then we shut the door, retreat into our own private hell.

Upstairs to the attic for me, to think again about love:
when it is all used up, when the passion is sunk
and betrayal is launched like a splendid ship
into the surreal sea, champagne slurped already, well,

all that is left is a stiff smile to the stranger
in your sitting-room, a small thank-you in the hall,
you taking the stairs two at a time to keep out of danger,
you drinking your choppy tea, grateful for good manners.

Notice

This is my second parking-ticket since her affair;
I can chart my progress from there to here.
Today in sub-zero temperatures, I got in quick,

under fourteen days, paid the penalty, £30 quid.
Last time, in the early bright yellow days,
I slipped past day fourteen and got smacked for sixty.

I thought sadly as I read out name on card, numbers
valid from, expires etc, this affair of hers
is costing me a fortune: Visa bills past the due date,

cheques turning up in the laundry basket, bank statements
lying about in the spare room; seventy pounds suddenly
found in the back pocket of black cords on their way

to charity. I've never been brilliant with money anyway,
but now that I've been switched – I've got much worse.
When we come to put the house on the market

I won't have a penny left in my black purse.

Husky

The voice of the husky in the snow
was hoarse, packed with loss
like snow that never melts.

Paw-prints that the wind blew
over, an old love letter,
fierce, ice-tight, blast.

If you'd never started out
wishing in the white, white snow,
you'd never be here now, howling, lost.

Her

I had been told about her.
How she would always, always.
How she would never, never.
I'd watched and listened
but I still fell for her,
how she always, always.
How she never, never.

In the small brave night,
her lips, butterfly moments.
I tried to catch her and she laughed
a loud laugh that cracked me in two,
but then I had been told about her,
how she would always, always.
How she would never, never.

We two listened to the wind.
We two galloped a pace.
We two, up and away, away, away.
And now she's gone,
like she said she would go.
But then I had been told about her –
how she would always, always.

Mirror, Mirror

She's holding back, now, my lover.
Been like this from summer to winter;
a long time now the dark one dark,

out in the bleak bleak time, bleached.
To give myself an extra edge,
I've cut my black hair, angular, chic.

Naked underneath our skin, dark hopes flutter;
I think it shows on my pale face –
that look, like someone loved

so gravely, she is betrayed. Our breasts meet
nipple to nipple, the milk sea ripples.
Gold round the edges of the oval mirror.

Out there is a calm sea, blue blue.
The gold balls roll into the big yonder.
Come out and breathe the salt sea air.

It's You and Me Baby All the Way
to the End of the Line

Yesterday you lied to me, my true love.
I knew you were, pretended you weren't –
that way maybe we could both be safer:
strolling along a disused railway line or
watching an old movie in our living-room.

Somehow yesterday it felt much better,
you lying into the home telephone;
your voice less sure now, less certain, softer.
And me here, miles away, snow on the hills,
listening to your voice down the long line

lying, love, like soft rain, lying again.
Today I can hear it still, picture, you, her
in some hotel, your voice, light in her ear.
Till I push you back further and further;
till I see nothing, just snow on the hills.

Clay

Better to catch things before they happen;
my face just before it smiles;
my heart the day before it breaks open.

Better to fancy blindly from a distance
than to fall into the chasm;
down there, where lives crack and spill.

Nobody – no other love – will likely
ever have the same slow charm,
that smile that was just about to happen.

Gone with the Wind

Everybody loves a nice smile
wide, and good teeth, white –
especially if you are black,
you learn to smile early.

But time enough already for all
that smiling, the jaws tire;
the snarl lurking behind the grin
gives the teeth ulcers.

Enough of the smiling.
If they don't like me without
the big grin and the white rolling eyes,
they can take a running jump in the wind.

The Staging of My Body

The cups have gone down four sizes;
four small cupids have sucked
and flown into the first day of spring.

Darling, the buds are opening again
like tiny cunts, dew wet and bursting
ready for absolutely anybody or anything.

The belly is flat now, stretch-marked
from the sudden loss of weight;
the navel is a shut eye in the dark.

The nipples – black figs; breasts, breadfruits.
Come tomorrow baby to the big ceremony
when I will look myself in the brown eye

and wave goodbye to the green eye,
and stand, take it now, with my right hand
on my left shoulder, my chin resting there,

my lips slightly open, wet, god yes, ready.

Model

I lay down on the wood table.
And the dark lay down beside me.
Think love while you are still able
when the world is in chaos, turmoil.

The face was painted onto mine.
My smile froze under the thick white.
Friends held my hands for auld lang syne;
and winter staggered into spring.

When the hard face is well shed,
do nothing; don't settle old scores.
To live bitter is to live dead.
Turn to life; keep the head.

Unforgiving Plaster

You won't let it go will you ever?
You'll just hold on to everything –
every wrong they did, your mum, your dad.
You won't let them forget; never, never.

The past is there to be raked over.
The dry bitter earth is rusty, cracked.
Now you can see it in your face,
hard cheek bones, thin mouth, furrowed brow.

You think you can forgive, forget
but you can't ever let it go.
You harden, your voice, brittle, breaks.
Your once lovely eyes, hard as flint.

If only you could get a boat
and load your cargo of resentment
and watch the boat sail away,
downriver, down the murky river on a summer's day.

Wax

When you lose your love
does it show on your face?
Can you hear it in your voice?
How many faces do you make up in your face?
When somebody asks you how you are,
how's the family, how's the kids,
does your face flatten or roughen or grow old
and is every second betrayed?
Is time frayed at the edges?
Does spring ever come back?
Is the blue of the sky or the blue of the sea
something you might see again?
And know that it is the perfect blue of the sky
the shimmering blue of the sea,
the very first day of spring?

Bronze

I really did think I could be somebody
different from this; a good head on my shoulders
an eye for an eye; a kiss for a kiss.

When my life turned upside down
and my face was stopped in time
I thought I could get off, let go, be myself.

But all of us are less than ourselves
in the days when we need to be more
and none of us can help ourselves

when love crashes down on us
and time runs out on us
and nothing can be done except what has been done.

The Mask of the Martyr

I wear the mask of the martyr,
a black hood over my ears.
I admit to feeling bitter.
I can't get over our years.

I trudge old streets in dismay.
Any day is martyr day.
See me cry on Wednesday,
hear me sigh on Saturday.

People always stare at a martyr.
The martyr knows and hoods the eyes.
Misery is there to barter for.
The broken heart is part disguise.

I've always been a wee misery,
always prone to soft self pity,
sadness is my one luxury.
Peel the hood back. Take the eyes.

Mid Life Mask

Everyone is so impatient.
I have to say, hold on I'm going
through my change of life.
It's no joke, don't expect me
to remember anything. I see
myself emerging through the Clyde tunnel
with a white face mask, my hair thick

as an animal's, sick to death
of the life at the tail end.
I crawl to the new one, on all fours.
Come through, wild, roaring,
my teeth fierce as a lion's.
So when somebody from the other life
says *I told you that already,*

what is the matter with you?
I don't say sorry. I am hot, fiery.
My face splits, fresh skin under the hard white.
I say, you are never the same woman twice.
The day is breaking; the light
in the dark sky is cracking through;
a new woman is out and about. Watch out.

Plaster

At last my lips are sealed;
and my eyes are shut tight.
No more talking; shielded
by the dark, the dumb black light.

Nothing left to talk about.
My face is tight on my face.
I won't shout; you won't shout.
Light will flood in; a state of grace.

Pencil, Knife

The light fails in the room in Edinburgh.
You draw an old map of love on my face.
You sharpen your pencil with a square blade.
Your white hair falls on your face.

You will draw me till the day I die, you say.
You will draw the face I had before I was born.
I slide down the armchair. I feel myself shift, change.
I am lost and found; my face is a fossil, a rock.

Light falls across your face; your heart is crushed.
Your pencil, gentle now, smudges, traces, creates.
I am taking shape before your eyes.
You draw the person inside me out. She says, *hush, hush*.

Things Fall Apart

My birth father lifted his hands above his head
and put the white mask of God on his handsome face.

A born-again man now, gone were the old tribal ways,
the ancestral village – African chiefs' nonsense, he says.

I could see his eyes behind the hard alabaster.
A father, no more real, still less real – not Wole Soyinka.

Less flesh than dark earth; less blood than red dust.
Less bone than Kano camels; less like me than Chinua Achebe.

Christianity had scrubbed his black face with a hard brush.
'You are my past sin, let us deliberate on new birth.'

The sun slips and slides and finally drops
into the swimming pool, in Nico hotel, Abuja; lonely pinks.

I knock back my dry spritzer, take in the songs
of African birds. I think he had my hands, my father.

The Wood Father

His hands were bark; his hair was leaves.
He stood tall and dark amongst the trees.
His arms waved in the wind, hello, goodbye;
words fluttered like birds from his eaves.

I couldn't tell if he loved me or not.
His eyes were darker than his barking hands,
nor if he wanted to meet again
in the dark forest, in the old red land.

His daughters, his sons, he would not name
or speak of them or anything they had done.
And when the rain fell down in the rainy season
he got up and moved across the forest floor

like a tree from Shakespeare; dragging his roots
all the way from Abuja to Enugu,
in the dead of night into the red of dawn.
Before he left, he gave me a name – Umeoja.

And I didn't point a twig or a finger.

A White African Dress

Yesterday, as I thought about what my father wore
that Sunday in Abuja when we first met;
a huge heron lit up my path through the woods
far from the river bank where the proud bird
usually stood, grave as a prayer.

It flew ahead of me away from the water –
its huge wings hesitating like a heavy heart –
through gold leaves fluttering from the bright trees.
He was dressed all in white, my father;
a long white African dress, ornate like lace,

repeating its pattern of intricate stitching.
The bright white lit up his black face.
My father chanted and ranted and prayed at my feet
creating wings with his hands; *Oh God Almighty*,
my hands, clasped tightly, nursed on my lap.

He held a black bible and waved it about
as he sang and danced around the hotel room
until the holy book opened its paper aeroplane wings
and my father flew off, his white dress trailing
like smoke in the sky, all the lovely stitches, dropping

dropping like silver threads on the dark red land.

Kano

I step back in time, old love,
along the hot dust, red road.
People – are they my people? –
drag their bare feet like camels

in this humped Sahara heat.
The air shoves its long hand
down my throat and pulls out
my back garden in Brackenbrae.

It puts its hands over my mouth,
whispers sweet new words in my ear.
My face is a bright mask now;
vivid stripes and streaks of colour.

I take Rabi Isma's cool, dark hand;
she leads me through the narrow alleys
of the oldest market, old love.
I am lost in time without you.

African Masks

One, Fertility Mask

Make me a baby Father – I saw you help the Sister here.
Make a baby before the end of the rainy season.
Hold my belly, here; talk my baby into coming.
Let me sing my baby a sweet song till morning.

You have a good face; your eyes see my longing.
Give me a boy who will see through holes in his chest.
I will dress him in a fibre dress and feed him my spirit.
When the bird eats the millet, it will fall down and die.

The fire will light itself and the bird will cook slowly.
Four trees will grow in the place I fall with child.
Feed me some sheep's liver; I will give it to my baby.
Open the earth for me; give the moon eyes to see me.

Father, don't let me lose my way; hear me.
The leopard pursues its prey. Morning breaks a day.
Give me a baby father before I break my heart.
Let me be with child, Father, before I am torn apart.

Two, Medicine Man

My father puts on his healing mask;
smells of cardamom and eucalyptus
rise from the carved wood.
'Heal me! Heal me!' I say softly.
He jumps up and kneels at my feet.
I can see his eyes through the mask.
He cooks words in a clay pot,
rubs them roughly into my forehead.
He shakes my head back and forth.
'You can walk through fire, you won't be burnt.
You can be tossed into the angry seas,
you won't drown. Don't even bother with
your hotel safe. You are protected.'
His hand covers my face. I can't breathe.
He takes off his healing mask and replaces
the father mask. 'Those were the beer-
drinking days. All the women loved me.'
A bird, a beautiful bird, lands on the table
and flies off. My father eats his hot pepper soup.
'All the women loved me. All the women loved me.
I played in a band. Scotland was lovely fun.
None of my children are dullards.
You are evidence of my past sin.
You have my genes.' One mask is on the table.
The waitress clears it up with the empty plates.
My father flies off. I say the words over again:
I can walk through fire. I won't get burnt.
I can get tossed into angry seas.
I won't drown. All the women love me.

Three, Rubber Girl

In the mirror, one face is lying
on top of the other, loose,
slightly unhinged. One pair of eyes
stares through to the other.
The face is more or less the same face.
I pull the thin curtains in the blue room.
The dark outside is the same dark.
My eyes close; bright colours spin
me to sleep in my father's country.
I dream the dream of the red road again.

I am made from the sticky resin of the rubber tree.
The spider that called me bastard child stuck to me.
I have a beautiful long neck, lovely large breasts.
When you insult me, I hold you tighter.
When you say I am the illegitimate child of low parents,
I kiss your cheeks, rub your back, whisper sweet things.
There is nothing you can do to me.
I am made from the sticky resin of the rubber tree.
All the men stick to me. I hold them tightly.

Four, Akweke

And oh what a glorious sight –
the water people that night!
I was the first to witness
the man slide into a woman's dress.
I saw the wild dancing –
grinding, swaying, twirling,
even the water was whirling
in the muddy flat land.
Oh they were lifting hands in the air,
shaking the hips, feet bare,
they were dancing in the dark.
I saw a pregnant woman with a penis
hidden behind her back. The whites of my eyes
were shining. The stars were sparkling.
The moon was a big drum in the sky.
The birds were singing like Ali Farka Toure.
Women with big head-dresses,
the wind billowing their costume dress,
swayed their bellies to the music.
Down by the water, even the boats were
changing – before my eyes – boats
into fish, then birds. Oh my.
Nobody looking at all surprised.
I am the first on earth to see.
I have seen people change before my eyes.
I have seen women change into men.
I have seen men change into women.
I have seen all this under the African skies.

Clay=Freedom

Just take a face, my face if you like
And give it another name

Just take the shape in your strong hands
And make it another shape

Just take my shape in your arms
And let it form another body

Just take the prints from my fingers
And give me a new pair of hands

Just take your hands and hold my new face
To your face and call me the other name.

Rubber

When I opened my eyes
my love was not the love of my life;
She was the love of somebody else's life;
'shit happens,' she said, 'that's life.'

When I closed my eyes,
my love kept fluttering under my eyelids:
all our years, our house, our kids,
our doting dog, our Charlotte Rhead jugs.

When I opened my eyes
I was younger, had lost three and a bit stone;
my heart lighter, my black hair shone.
Keys in a new door; the deeds done.

A new double bed: enough said.

Rubble

What was the thought that I just had in my head?
It's gone and I want to grab it. It brought to mind.
The world is in bits and things smash and crash.
It was small, inconsequential? Or, or,
was it something not worthy of the red admiral
I just saw on the grass. Something crucial?
Change the record? Maybe that: stop playing
the broken heart. The world outside is breaking

apart. Pull yourself together, maybe? Something
like that. I can't be sure. Thoughts crumble
and disintegrate and disappear. Cucumber for
my eyes, remember get cucumber? I used to have order
in my house, my head. Now I can't remember
a thing I've said. It's all a whirl and a swirl,
a gush and a gutter, a flood, a mud spill.
Goodness – it's all mess and clutter and rubble

in my soft head. All I want is the dear old bed.
Downstairs – damp proof men and the radio blaring.
Upstairs – the tiles are falling off the roof.
One day I hope for somebody kind, somebody
who would not make me feel I was losing my mind.
Somebody who wouldn't mind where I put what
or what I forgot. Or what else is there? I can't remember.
Somebody what? Somebody who? Dear oh dear, somebody you.

End of the Line

These last few days before I leave
are most peculiar;
my phone has sunk to the bottom of the sea
and I am underwater.

Every helping friend asks me to speak up
or repeat myself:
'Can't hear you, you are muffled.'
My line underwater swims like an eel.

These days I can't tell what I really feel.
Bubbles come out of my mouth.
Who knows what lies at the end of the line?
Somebody shouts help. Somebody dials 999.

The police turn up at my house and insist on a search.
My voice gets softer and softer.
My words are thick, mud, slime, seaweed.
Somebody catch me. Pull me up.

New Old Past

After all the rubble and the fallout,
when the wires went and the water flooded,
after all our past and all our dead future,
I can't remember who I was or where
we were; I think we were going for supper.

And it was to be an ordinary supper
before the water and the mud-slinging,
before your eyes opened and mine fluttered –
like that single red admiral we saw
years ago on the pile of rubble,

remember? How beautiful, how bright?
One or two things stick out from that night.
Of course there were the twin herons next day,
years later, standing frozen in the heron way,
staring cool and quiet from the fake island.

Or no, some things just now are flooding in.
There was the deer, remember, the red deer
with the haughtiest stare in Strathfarrar.
But all that was before; this is after,
and now, old lover, we are further away

from the red deer and the red admiral,
from the heron and the horse and the massive spider
that appeared that night in Ty Newydd,
or any of our years, when I said 'Jesus Mince,
that's a huge spider!' and you guffawed.

But it's all gone now, floating down the river.
The past is a horse swimming; a red admiral landing,
a heron's hard look back. The past is a soft touch.
The past is a bony hand coming out of the rubble.
The past is powdery snow melting in my mouth.

George Square

My seventy-seven-year-old father
put his reading glasses on
to help my mother do the buttons
on the back of her dress.
'What a pair the two of us are!'
my mother said, 'Me with my sore wrist,
you with your bad eyes, your soft thumbs!'

And off they went, my two parents
to march against the war in Iraq,
him with his plastic hips, her with her arthritis,
to congregate at George Square where the banners
waved at each other like old friends, flapping,
where'd they'd met for so many marches over their years,
for peace on earth, for pity's sake, for peace, for peace.

I Kin See Richt thru My Mither

My mother always said you could see right through me,
and on winter days she was the first to notice
if I was peally wally, when I looked like her father's
peeweet, his miner's singlet, the colour of lapwing's wings.

My voice plummeting or flying too high was picked up,
if I was peesie-weesie or perskeet, she'd remember
the names of the girls in her class and recite them
like a lovely kirk service, how those eight tight friends

played peever, and how my mother's hair back then
travelled the length of her back, thick-thick
until it had to be shaved off, Oh god, bloody awful.
On days when my wings were grey and still,

my mother's stories of herself as a girl flew around
our house like Uncle Wullie's, from Lochgelly, birds
in his home-made aviary, such pretty colours, chests puffed
as Aunt Ag's puff pastry, my mother brought the colour back,

to my winter face. Stories of mine shafts and pewter tubs,
the long lengths of miners' backs washed for a penny;
the days when the past was so dreamy it seemed it was lived
by somebody else; the days we savoured her past like ghosts.

Childhood, Still

The sun is out and so is childhood – remember
how the summer droned its song forever.

Three small girls tumble down the steep hill.
Grass skips, gust makes their skirts frill.

A wee boy scoots towards the big blue loch.
His fishing net bigger than his baw face.

It's hot; there's a breeze like a small caught breath.
This is it; these are the days that never stop.

Childhood ticks, tocks, ticks. Metronome.
Speaking clock. Sand glass. Time bomb.

A boy kicks a ball through a window, smashes
a gaping hole, but this is childhood still

where big things grow small: small as a petal
or a freckle on a face, a speckle

on an egg, or as small as a tadpole,
small as the space where the ball missed the goal,

as dot to dot, as a crumb of Mrs Jack's cake,
small as the silver locket around her neck.

The long grass whines in the high wind.
Away in the distance, the church bells chime.

Childhood ticks, tocks, ticks. Metronome.
Speaking clock. Sand glass. Time bomb.

Suddenly: the clatter of boots in the street.
The sob of a white van speeding away.

The cries of a small boy alone in a stairwell.
This is childhood; this is childhood as well.

The policeman caught by the Candyman.
A town's sleep murdered by the Sandman.

There goes the janitor, the teacher, the priest,
clergyworker, childminder, careworker. *Wheesht.*

The auntie, the uncle, the father, the mother;
opening and closing and opening the door.

Childhood ticks, tocks, ticks. Metronome.
Speaking clock. Sand glass. Time bomb.

Oh There she goes.
Oh There she goes.
Peerie heels and pointed toes.
Look at her feet. She thinks she's neat.
Black stockings and dirty feet.

Remember the toadstool, the promise of a chrysalis,
the taste of lemon bonbons, the taste of liquorice.

The past keeps calling the children back.
Number six: pick up sticks. Tick tack, Tick tack.

The clock hands crawl, August's slow talk.
Autumn comes: the snap and crackle of amber leaves.

There's a brand new friend waiting in the school,
a gleam in her eye, ready for Tig or marbles.

Skip, skop to the barber's shop, Keepie-Uppie, Kerbie.
Bee Baw Babbity, Following Wee Jeannie.

Green peas and Barley. Okey Kokey. My mummy told me.
Stotty. Peever. Thread the needle. The Big Ship sails.

This is childhood, let it be childhood still.

Old Tongue

When I was eight, I was forced south.
Not long after, when I opened
my mouth, a strange thing happened.
I lost my Scottish accent.
Words fell off my tongue:
eedyit, dreich, wabbit, crabbit
stummer, teuchter, heidbanger,
so you are, so am ur, see you, see ma ma,
shut yer geggie or I'll gie you the malkie!

My own vowels started to stretch like my bones
and I turned my back on Scotland.
Words disappeared in the dead of night,
new words marched in: ghastly, awful,
quite dreadful, *scones* said like *stones*.
Pokey hats into ice cream cones.
Oh where did all my words go –
my old words, my lost words?
Did you ever feel sad when you lost a word,
did you ever try and call it back
like calling in the sea?
If I could have found my words wandering,
I swear I would have taken them in,
swallowed them whole, knocked them back.

Out in the English soil, my old words
buried themselves. It made my mother's blood boil.
I cried one day with the wrong sound in my mouth.
I wanted them back; I wanted my old accent back,
my old tongue. My dour soor Scottish tongue.
Sing-songy. I wanted to *gie it laldie*.

Piano 4 P.M.

The music lifts – up and up and up –
my son's scales,
trails his long brown fingers.

It is so particular. Doh ray me.
He sits like time held still
on the red piano stool.

Fah soh la. The scales linger on his shoulders,
circle his childhood, Te Doh,
and saunter down the hall,

to float above me
in the kitchen cooking his dinner.
The music lifts the lids.

Biding time; holding the moment well.
In the interval, the strange space
between notes,

I chop onions. I stir and wait.
Taste and pause. I grind some pepper.
Sprinkle some sea salt. He starts again.

And in they come, the children
from another time; lifting their skirts, running
by the dark river.

And the bells of the past, they ring and ring;
an old woman remembers how she used to dance,
waltzing, waltzing into the night air.

And the night waves rish and crash and falter.
And the rocks are always bare and glistening.
My son plays *Arioso in F*

away into the future.
I can hear him grow up,
up and off, off and up.

I can see us
in the space between the bars:
mother and son.

Here we come and go.
My boy will become a man.
The light will see the dark.

The music flowing now
sweeps and turns,
rising and falling, innocent and knowing.

Pushing out its long limbs.
The dance of the bones.
It yearns and swings,

through the heart of our home.
I hold my wooden spoon mid-air
like a proud conductor.

Tears fall down my face like notes.

High Land

I don't remember who kissed who first,
who touched who first, who anything to whom.
All I remember in the highland night –
the sheep loose outside,
the full moon smoking in the sky –
was that you led me and I led you.
And all of a sudden we were in a small room
in a big house with the light coming in
and your legs open; mine too.
And it was this swirling, twirling thing.
It's hard to fasten it down;
it is hard to remember what was what –
who was who when the wind was coming in.

Out There

Now you are out there in the wild seas;
your small boat battering at the big waves.
The night is darker than you'd have ever believed;
each cruel wave soaks you right through.

There is no lighthouse light, no rescue party.
The small moon is shrunk like a dehydrated brain.
The stars are shattered empty bottles of wine.
And you are out there alone, my own one.

And there is nothing I can do for you,
I can't throw you a line; I can't get help.
I'm stuck here shivering on the shore watching
your dark boat – your bleak bow braving the loss.

You cling to the wheel, sway from side to side.
Waves, the height of houses, smash and toss.

The Road You Take (Unfinished)

Who ever knew you could grieve the living so deeply
that you just down the road and off to the left
could feel so very far away; and on a day like today

the past we shared feels flimsy like a dress bereft
after a party when the body has climbed out of it
and it is left lying carelessly on the bedroom floor.

Or worse – it feels like it didn't happen at all,
not the way we thought it did and maybe I didn't know you
not really, not the way I thought I did.

You have left this big hole like a manhole
in a dark childhood street, the stank pulled up;
strange things crawling way down underneath.

I am afraid of chucking new people down the hole.
Of forgetting you and all the things we ever said.
Of rushing down the slick new road, slipping on the bend.

I didn't ever think – did you – that it would so neatly end?

Old Aberdeen

You'll never see what I'll give you
Out in the open country; the light coming in from the North Sea.
You'll never see what I'll give you
Up in the north, growing old under the lights of old Aberdeen.
You'll never see what I'll give you
A stone door opening to sunshine, the corn rigs the barley oh,
You'll never see, you'll never know
A song for every single day my love – Maxwellton braes are bonny.
You'll never see what I'd give you
Not now my lovely lassie oh.

Promise

Remember, the time of year
when the future appears
like a blank sheet of paper
a clean calendar, a new chance.
On thick white snow

you vow fresh footprints
then watch them go
with the wind's hearty gust.
Fill your glass. Here's tae us. Promises
made to be broken, made to last.

Eleven Chances

You write like a dream.
Your eyes are dreamy,
the blue sea in them.
I dream you often,
standing sturdy, firm
on the old dream land.

You give good advice –
a path of small stones
I can follow some
day I understand.
In the slow mean time
you hold my hard hand.

Two Autumns

Last autumn, the windscreen wipers sliced the windows
of my big car in the pouring rain, over and over,
folding in on each other, crossing themselves in prayer.
My glasses blurred, my seatbelt never ever on
I drove one-handed, through the driving rain,
and suddenly turned up at my own door, again and again.

This autumn, the trees are a girl with no clothes on.
The trees have slowly been undressing their leaves.
The ground of burnished orange is a big surprise.
Spring has pushed its way up through autumn: Here I am
open-eyed, beginning, beginning all over again,
astonished at the naked girl in the exhilarating rain.

Dream Pier

Dream of me riding the horse you galloped as a girl –
the one that rode onto the ferry

just as the floor was rising up, in the days when
horses rode the wild sea.

Dream of us swimming in the crazy sea,
our wet hair dark as seals

just as they rise up from the salt water
sleek, slippery clever.

Dream of you, dream of me, and the old country,
strolling in the heather.

Dream of the years falling off, and the rainy weather.
Then dream of us as girls,

Bold girls who become black horses, black horses who bolt
the stable one dark night.

Donkey

Us two hee-hawing to ourselves out in the cobbles
when the moon slipped like a girl across the sky
and the shining stars were apples or potatoes.
Us two snorting and stamping and slapping up a love
when the day broke across our bare backs
and steam flared from our wide nostrils.
Us two stamped out that bright, cold January day –
slapped the knackered wood door down
and galloped, like stories, across the green grass.
And we couldn't, we couldn't stop ourselves.
Us two biting, kicking; swinging our big fat asses
sinking our glad hooves into the soft grasses.
Us two going like this: *he haw he heee heeeee heeeeee.*
Until they came for us, they did, so they bloody did,
put us back in the yard – cobbled, cold; to grow old.

But aw oh ah yes it was worth every blade of grass,
every fresh mouth of pure air, every singing tree.
Us two would never have not – would we – broke out, scot-free.

Baggage

Dark, the days when the ships came slowly in,
carrying the baggage from the old past,
old love letters, promises long since past.

Icy cold it was that winter morning,
thick fog blurred the ship mast.
The ship humped in like a hurt already cast.

You had to go and pick it up. You pushed in,
signed the slip for your wicker chest,
and trudged the roads and miles back west,

carrying your past on your back, late morning,
like an animal carries what it needs to its den.
The old loch at your side, lapping: *Ye ken*

this – it is not as heavy it might be.
You step to your small house in the new light.

Moon Mask

Dark now, try to sleep my darkling.
The moon up there is night-shy
And hiding, the stars are secrets;
The sky is a vast grey blanket.

Nobody knows how much we hide darkling
Hidden in our house till morning,
The things we never ever said;
The things that are best forgotten.

Life Mask

When the senses come back in the morning,
the nose is a mouth full of spring;
the mouth is an earful of birdsong;
the eyes are lips on the camomile lawn;
the ear is an eye of calm blue sky.

When the broken heart begins to mend,
the heart is a bird with a tender wing,
the tears are pear blossom blossoming,
the shaken love grows green shining leaves.
the throat doesn't close, it is opening

like a long necked swan in the morning,
like the sea and the river meeting,
like the huge heron's soaring wings:
I sat up with my pale face in my hands
and all of a sudden it was spring.